Martha Armstrong-Hand's
Living Dolls

a picture story
by David Hand

Martha Armstrong-Hand's Living Dolls

A Picture Story by David Hand

Calligraphy by Martha Armstrong-Hand

Printed in the United States of America
ISBN: 0-87588-199-8

This picture story is dedicated to all those grown-ups who love the little people who inhabit the doll world.

Author's tribute

This tale is a fantasy - a mirage of imagination. It's about Martha Armstrong-Hand, an incredible talent who sculptures little people - little porcelain people.

Her training began many, many years ago in Germany. During the war years as a young girl, circumstances forced her to barter her budding artistic talent for a crust of bread. She was fortunate in being able to escape the Holocaust and to finally find a warm and welcome home in the United States.

Throughout her many years of continuing development, she has gradually emerged as a most outstanding sculptor, second to none in her chosen creative field, and is even now continuing to create masterpieces of the doll world for collectors. Her sculptures are much sought after, and for those who have been fortunate enough to obtain one of her limited editions, they are considered most favored indeed.

I am very proud to have become the husband of Martha Armstrong-Hand. Certainly, without her continued help this book would never have been possible.

David Hand, story teller.

A Cast of Characters

Michael

Juanita

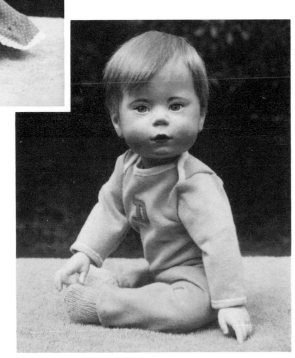

Carol

Kadra

Damien

Once upon a time there was a Grandma who — no, that wouldn't be true — <u>not</u> "Once upon a time" — Grandmas are <u>forever</u>, thank goodness.

This is a story about a special grandma who sculpts beautiful children for doll collectors. Her granddaughter, Beth, teasingly calls her "Grandma Gepetto" except she never really thought the dolls would ever grow long noses, like Pinocchio. Grandma doesn't mind being called "Grandma Gepetto" because her dolls are so much a part of her.

Beth would watch Grandma by the hour, forgetting sometimes to go out and play with the neighbor children. She loved the little babies in their gay, cheerful costumes almost as much as Grandma did.

One day she asked, "Grandma, do you ever wish your doll babies were real live people like me?"

Grandma thoughtfully replied, "Do you know, Beth, deep down inside I secretly feel they really do come to life because I put a little of me into each one of their tiny sculptured parts."

Beth remembered her dream about the new porcelain babies that Grandma was then finishing. Looking up into Grandma's smiling face, Beth exclaimed, "I had a kind of funny bad dream last night. Want to hear about it, Grandma?" Grandma encouragingly agreed, "Well, yes, if it wasn't too awful, Beth dear."

Beth breathlessly hurried on with her dream story before Grandma could change her mind. "Well, after you had tucked me into bed and I was fast asleep, your little doll children <u>really</u> did come <u>alive</u> and were very naughty. Grandma, they tied me up tight so that I couldn't stop them from getting into mischief."

"With no mother to scold them, they started making a mess of our nice clean living room."

Grandma gasped, "I just can't believe it!"

Beth, being encouraged to proceed with all the "very naughty" details, excitedly continued, "And guess what, Grandma. Michael was playing cowboy, and was riding his rocking horse like crazy, acting awful smart - as he always does —"

"— when bonk! — and good for him too.
He was all of a sudden bucked high in the
air and dumped right flat onto the floor.
That sure taught him where to 'get off'.
— That's a joke, Grandma."

"Goodness me.—Juanita didn't know which end was up. Can you imagine her trying to sit up at the dinner table like <u>that</u>!"

"Now here was something—Kadra rummaging into Mother's dresser drawers. These days, babies just don't seem to understand anything much."

"Guess what, Grandma,— when Kadra got all dressed up, she just sat there. Do you think maybe she wanted to feel real grown-up?"

"Damien and Carol didn't know any better
— they played house with Daddy's books."

"Michael was so cute, but he just didn't put the wastepaper back into the basket when he stopped clowning."

"When Carol got tired of playing with Daddy's books, she thought she could knit herself a sweater."

"Instead of that, Grandma, Carol wrapped herself up like a mummy, and Damien couldn't decide how to go about unraveling her."

"Pulling a pillow apart sure does have its feather problems. Kadra got herself into real trouble."

"I really tried to warn them when I saw the button jar right at the edge of the table —"

"—It was too late!
It's no wonder that Juanita was hiding."

"When Carol and Kadra came to the rescue, everybody had the surprise of their lives — Mr. Caterpillar had come out of the flower pot."

"Inch by inch old Mr. Caterpillar tried to escape the curious crawlers, hot on his trail."

" They _got_ him."

"Would you believe it, Grandma! Mr. Caterpillar became the most beautiful butterfly I have ever seen."

"When Mr. Butterfly flew out the window, Kadra, Damien, Juanita, Carol and Michael waved and waved good-bye until they couldn't see him anymore!"

"Wasn't that a lovely dream, Grandma?
I do love every one of your darling dolls."

"Know what? All of us love you most
of all — you're the bestest Grandma
that – ever – was!"

...And Grandma's dolls lived
happily ever after.

Documentation of the production of "America's future" dolls, by Martha Armstrong-Hand.

All of the five dolls pictured in the foregoing flight of fancy are portraits of 9-month-old babies of assimalated ancestries. Juanita is Mexican-Indian. Michael is Jewish-Brazilian. Kadra is Afro-Cherokee. Carol is Asian-Irish. Damien is German-English. Each has been made completely of porcelain bisque, and each has 19 component parts with 16 separate leather-lined joints held together by springs, swivels, hooks, bars and rings; all made of stainless steel. Their hair is made of nylon, hand-stitched on a silk cap; their eyes, hand-painted. They were designed, sculpted, engineered for human mobility, also costumed by Martha Armstrong-Hand.

They are approximately 13 inches high, and were produced in limited editions of 10. Production of the first doll of each of the series took a total of about 300 hours. Final completion of the dolls required three years.

The nape of their necks are incised "Martha Armstrong-Hand" with copyright "MA-H" imprint, and showing the year produced. The specific edition number of each doll of the limited editions is recorded at the same spot. Also, there are incised "MA-H" markings on the rear shoulder pieces. The costumes carry the cloth labels "Martha Armstrong-Hand". They are certified NIADA (National Institute of American Doll Artist) dolls.

About the Author

Every so often a fellow comes along with an idea, bursting to crack open its eggshell. David Hand found himself in the right hen house at the right time, and this book is the result of his hatched idea — young, vigorous and anxious to be accepted by qualified egg-watchers.

This is David Hand's second time around in expressing himself with picture books. His first, Today is Yesterday, Tomorrow, was the result of the successful collaboration with poetess Nancy Martin.

All of his working life has been devoted to tickling funny bones — 10 years "B.D." (before Disney), animating and directing pictures in New York, 15 years with early Disney, helping him to hatch his colossal egg, animating and directing inumerable short subjects, Supervising Director of Snow White and Bambi, Production Supervisor on Dumbo, Fantasia and Pinocchio, before leaving for England to become Managing Director of the then embryonic cartoon industry for the J. Arthur Rank organization.

Now semi-retired, he is secretary and business manager for his wife, Martha, giving his full support to further her ever-expanding talent.